Syncere's Soliloquy

Syncere

BookLeaf
Publishing

India | USA | UK

Presentation by *BookLeaf Publishing*

Web: www.bookleafpub.com

E-mail: info@bookleafpub.com

ISBN: 9789395271172

First edition 2022

DEDICATION

I dedicate this to those who don't know how much power words can wield. I dedicate this to those who suffer under the weight of their own expectations. I dedicate this to those who have loved and lost. And above all, I dedicate this to those who, despite every obstacle in their path to self discovery, found peace.

Sincerely Thine.

Sincerely Mine.

Syncerely Ours.

ACKNOWLEDGEMENTS

I want to thank our Father and Creator for helping me find my voice, yet again. Without you, Jehovah, I'm mere dust.

Those who know I love them should remain secure in that knowledge. If you have to question it ... this section is not for you.

My mother, Big D, will never go without mention. You are the perfect verse over a tight beat. Crys-a-lis & Riner-face - you complete me. Shaad, you had me at "hello". Kaleb, my future began when you were born.

The Varner Garden and the Royal Rhone Estate - you are the homes where my heart resides. Mariah, you're my hero and the gift of your friendship is more than I deserve. Naomi, my little sister, you've found me when I had forgotten I was lost. Jill, you've shown me what it means not only to grow, but to thrive. Ma and Dad - thank you for your undeserved, all encompassing love. To the next 39 years!

Honorable mentions to the men who inspire me, challenge me, and give me grief & joy. Thank you, CJ, for inspiring me. Thank you, Selom, for saving me. Thank you, Sheed, for challenging me. Thank you, Brian, for all of the above.

To those we lost this round, DJ Williams and Alexis Katrice Jones, hopefully you'll get to read this one day.

And to anyone who has been or become one of my readers, I appreciate you. Out of all the books in all the world ... here you are reading mine. You're special to me and I love you.

Special shoutout to the Bookleaf staff - it's only possible to print if someone is willing to print it. You have my eternal thanks.

PREFACE

Finding my voice in a world that's full of self importance and rhetoric was a happy accident. If I can create just a bit of beauty in the void of existence, let it be through the written word.

- Syncerely, The Author

FRACTURED FAIRYTALE

Gather round while I regale
You with my fractured fairytale
My humble origins is where
I will begin and go from there
Once upon a time a Queen
Gave birth to 3 young girls- the King
Unfortunately, would not be
The Knight the precious girls would need
The oldest one was always nice
The middle girl was full of spice
The youngest was naive in life
Not all, it seems, would end in strife
Beautiful, each on their own
None wanted to ascend the throne
Content to forge their own paths forward
The standards for themselves not lowered
The eldest two became quite strong
Though Princes did not come along
None stood the trials to win their hearts
Suitors found wanting from the start
The youngest watched and learned her role
She tried to glean both big and small
Lessons that would serve her well
And prayed she'd live long enough to tell
Fables great, details minute
But truths no one would dare dispute
She'd face monsters all by herself

Slain at the expense of mental health
She'd take the narrowed road ahead
At times, devoid of strength, she'd shed
Tears for her stolen innocence
Afraid she'd never gain the chance
To find a love untainted by
Fear and confusion of years gone by
She chose, her armor, to forge anew
Her sword, her pen, was then imbued
With capabilities astounding
Tales of villains & heroes resounding
First, in her head then on the page
The outpouring of all her rage
The healing came once she accepted
A slight revision, her course corrected
It came as almost a surprise
So clear, once she opened up her eyes
For she was, from birth, to be tasked
With recording all that came to pass
She may have failed as sister or daughter
She refused to fail them as the Author

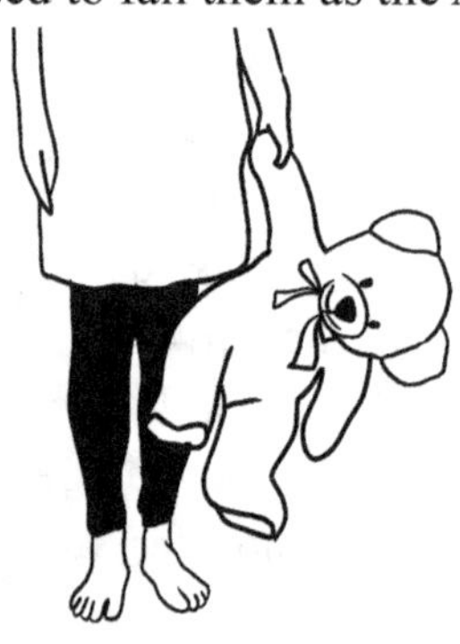

IRONY

Irony.
That's what life is.
A never ending journey of irony.
Slaving away to earn our freedom.
Hiding who we are, whilst begging to be seen.
Running, eyes wide shut, into new situations that
have the same parameters
of what we're running from.
Finding someone to be with, but never feeling
more alone than when they are by your side.
Dying to live.
Living to die.
Irony.

I can think of no bigger irony than love.
That exquisite pain.
Pain that can be either your utter destruction
or your saving grace.
It can break you, yet put you back together.
It can make you hate someone
you once couldn't live without.
Giving of yourself, only to be taken for granted.
Confusing yet clarifying, devastating but
uplifting. Satisfying, yet can leave you empty.
Life is ironic. Love is ironic.
We live our lives governed by irony.

LOSS

Moving forward is an arduous task at times
Trying to follow a narrow path of blurry lines
Clouded by fear and tears of unfair loss
And the emotional onslaught of unpaid costs
Taxes tacked on by inherent sin
Subtraction of worth multiplied from within
Addition of stress caused from sickness & pain
Divided by thought processes weighing the strain
They say a life well lived is the ultimate goal
But those left behind can attest that the soul
The person with the life path that came to an end
Is infinitely painful for family and each friend
A more delicate balancing act is unknown
Of both moving forward, yet moving on alone
It's a greeting you won't experience soon enough
Or a last goodbye said that felt way too tough
Two arms devoid of a warm embrace
One heart divided by loneliness you now face
Yes, there is a beautiful hope for days to come
Presently, though, you may feel
both hurt and numb
Though the length of a life
Can be measured in years
The depth of loss of that loved one
Is measured in tears
So each day I awake,
I pray I can hold on 'til the end
Until such a time when I can be with you again

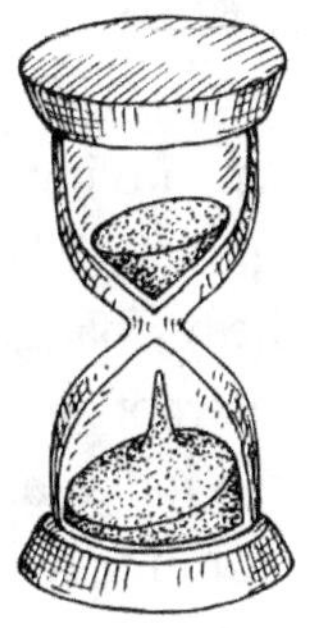

HURT

I am gracious. I am kind.
But to my flaws I am not blind.
I do my best, with my goals,
To keep moving toward
And strive to put my best foot forward.
I have heavy baggage, yes.
It's often the root cause of stress,
But I need no judgment doled out.
I have no room for fears & doubts.
I can struggle by myself
And I didn't ask you for your help.
Who made you both my judge and jury?
I don't need your insincere worry.
You're not my father, mother, sibling, or friend?
Then, please, don't think of me again.
Your words, they cut me, & looks of disdain
Hold me hostage to emotional pain.
I thought that I had moved on and yet,
Sure enough, I'm sitting here bereft.
I thought I had finally shown
Growth of character alone.
I can't be held to a standard higher
Than what I've set out to acquire.
You'll have to mind my imperfection,
And don't take it as a deflection.
I'm more than plenty self aware;
Reflect on yourself, if you dare.

I give myself over to the care
Of a loving Creator who will spare
Me from anyone who puts on airs,
(With fake concern then disappears).
I can forgive and hold you in my heart.
I can love you from miles apart.

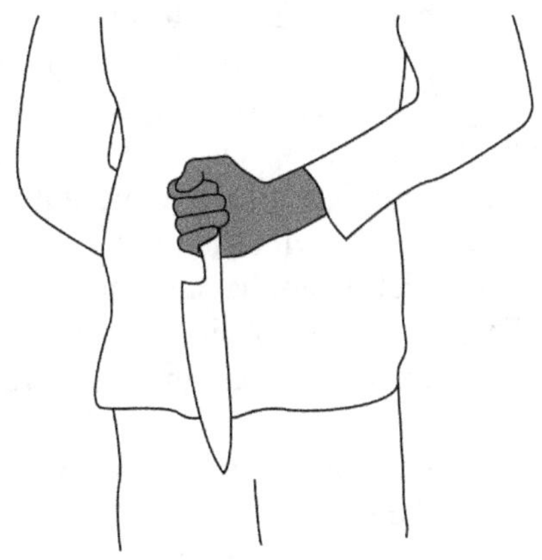

ALEXIS KATRICE JONES

From birth we could all see your worth.
Smart and sweet and full of joy.
Humble and full of light.
I don't think we ever had a real fight.
Fiercely loyal and protective as hell.
I never once doubted, in this world,
you'd fare well.
This feeling is surreal-
it can't be your final farewell.
AlleyCat or Kat Rice-
nicknames from when you were small.
You would laugh and joke along with us all.
A model's looks with the purest of hearts.
In your eyes, reflected the sun, moon, and stars.
There's so much I didn't get to say.
Every single person who knew you
Has been dreading this day.
There's absolutely no ransom
we wouldn't have paid
To ensure you'd endure, but to rest you are laid.
You were a testament to kindness.
You never changed how you move.
If nothing else, you've never had to prove
What we already knew to be true.
You deserved the world.
Ours are slightly smaller now without you in it.
There's not a word to describe the pure pain
Of knowing not another person
will be able to gain
Access to the light of your smile.
The only comfort we know is

You get to rest for a while.
But I know one day you will have another chance
To astound us all
with the greatest gift we can recall.
A chance to hear you laugh again.
A chance to hold you close.
A chance to tell you all the things
We love about you most.
And you won't have to suffer.
You won't be alone.
With those who love you there is always a home.
You're a daughter and sister
Who will be treasured forever.
A niece and auntie, and for added measure,
A friend who left the deepest impression.
In your absence we'll try
to remember the lessons.
So sleep, our dear princess.
You've done all you can for now.
We'll keep you close in mind
And remember we'll meet again, somehow.

JUNETEENTH

I am guilty. Guilty of living this life.
No lunch counters turned me away.
No blatant slurs to my face did they say
No "Whites Only" signs kept me at bay
No slave labor without the pay
This life, by comparison, bears no strife.

I am haunted. Haunted by our history.
The chains and whips across our skin
Being punished without sin
Sacrificed in wars, we could not win
Waiting for life without bondage to begin
Our history's justice was blind indeed

I am penitent. For my privileged existence
From being shipped overseas
Bound and shackled amid many bodies
Worked in fields; hands blistered & feet bloody
Close encounters lead to
bodies swinging from trees
My penitence lie in escaping a slave's sentence

NO MORE

The way women are treated at times
Never fails to bring tears to my eyes
First, you beat her and call her a whore
Then slap her down
when she won't give you more
She tries to stay strong
She doesn't fight back
So you take advantage and keep up the attack
She'll scream and cry- maybe send you to jail
Then be the first to post under your bail
She loves you unconditionally, without restraint
And does it with nary an utterance or complaint
It's time to stand up - tell him where he can go
Next time he says "jump" you tell him "no"
Own your beauty and intellect
Remember you're strong
Don't allow him to continue to do you wrong
A friend is a sister
who is born for times of stress, indeed
You have support in me if you're ever in need

SUCH IS LOVE

Your eyes.
I can see my unborn child and almost feel the
first kicks in my womb as I look into them.
Your nose.
I imagine I am that life sustaining air that you
inhale and exhale.
Your lips.
I imagine then kissing and caressing my earlobe,
as I spout sweet sonnets upon your listening ear.

And yet as I pick up a pen to express
this tempest of emotions…
I find myself devoid of anything to write.
Everything I thrive on, my very existence,
Fail to remain contained to
mere sentiment & trite words.
So I go forth and seek your face, yearning for
your touch alone until ..
I find you. With another.

My eyes.
My vision is blurred and I stumble through
darkness, blinded by tears.
My lips.
Animalistically tortured and strangled are the
sounds that emit from the depths of my soul.
My heart.

I feel it searing and tearing apart from the white-hot pain spreading through my chest.

Such is Love.

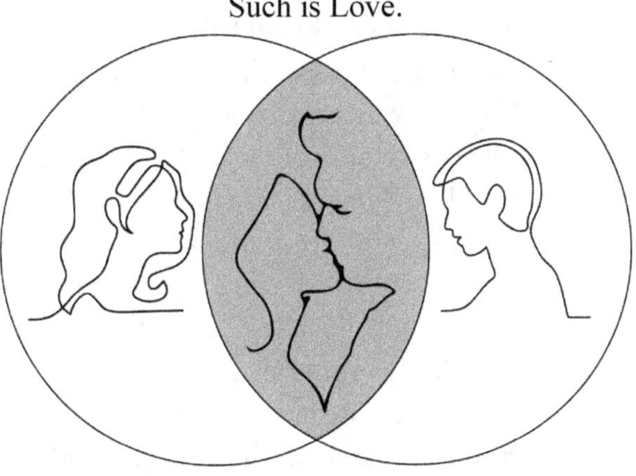

YESTER-ME, YESTER-YOU

I fell in love with yesterday's version of you.
You were the guy I could always run to.
Escaping my insecurities and fears,
Wiping away my doubts and tears.
But today's version of me can clearly see
My judgment was clouded.
I'm somewhat confounded;
How did you manage to hide
Behind those gilded lies?
Pretty prose full of holes
With intent, I surmise.
Exceedingly cunning, surprisingly kind.
Artificially sweet in most ways
Memory calls to mind.
But you've given me a rare gift
In abusing my trust.
And only God can judge you,
So instead I'll simply just
Level up, push on, and stand on my own.
Two feet planted, ten toes down
And ascend to my throne.
I wish you the very best that life has to give.
Respectfully, you'll regret my loss
As long as you live.

DO NOT DISTURB

You shoot your shot
After a shot or two of henny
A plethora of unwanted advances
I've got plenty
And I'm more than plenty tired
Of recycled lines and quips
The ads for sugar babies
And false promises of trips
Around the world
If I were your girl
Would you show me the clear respect
Of not sending DMs or flirty texts
To the next pretty face
With a fat ass and slim waist
It's a waste of my time
Actually, both yours & mine
To entertain
A fleeting fantasy of me that
Crosses your brain
You'd have to be someone
clinically labeled as insane
Or blind to miss the fact that I shine
I'm divine and I'm real
My immaculate flow? Ideal
And that's without getting tossed
Match my energy or get lost
You can't handle these curves

If you can't handle my words
Ayo boss,
I'm more than a woman
More of a legend
And the dividing of these thighs
Is akin to ascending straight to heaven
So what's the lesson?
Find it in yourself to know that wealth
Won't afford you the blessing
That is getting to my heart
Before I tear your world apart
I'm investing in much more than pretty lies
And unfulfilled mommy issues
So it should come as no surprise
That tears for second chances are met
Only with pity and tissues
I'm not in the business of fixing
Broken men
Mama didn't raise no fool
I apply pressure until emerges a gem
I don't mind taking my time to put
You through the wringer
And you got me twisted if you think
I'm a stage 5 clinger
I'm young, but I'm ready
As a rock I am steady
Try my best not to be petty
But it's clear to see you're not the
One for me if you think that for

One second a weak text and a smile
Will make me the next female you
Disappoint for a while
Until you find yourself repeating
Old habits.
Getting loose off the Goose and
Swiping right
I'll save you the trouble and
Simply bid you goodnight

SLEEPING BEAUTY

I have loved before. I guess.
Let's call a spade, a spade;
It was a mess.
So I loved until I lost, but the thought did cross
My mind it could be
That our timing was just off.
We crashed and we burned but my
Lessons were well learned.
When all was said and done
I blamed me. Solely.
I figured someone that fine? Someone all mine?
He was no Highlander,
but there could only be One.
For the first time, in a long time I might add,
I dreamt of someone else.
Let's call him- you know what? No.
We're not naming names, because y'all?
This man came to play no games.
He seeped into my subconscious,
And he drove me insane.
And it may not have been first,
But he was glad that he came.
His eyes were so blue
They looked right through to the core of me.
And I bet he could tell the sex
Of our future progeny.
Honestly, I wouldn't mind pairing

My first name with his last.
The thirst so real, his girth ideal-
It may just be quarter past time to move on.
Shed the proverbial shroud,
Get back to living out loud.
Yes, my 1st love is gone.
But life is about continuing forward
Until you reach the end of your set course.
Of course, I'll always miss him.
His presence was no small loss.
But I can't deviate from the plan for me
'Cause I am a boss.
And the man who interrupts my dreams
Is really a toss.
The dice could be loaded. I'm not easily goaded
But it's nice to have dreams
Instead of nightmares come true.
It'd be a pleasant surprise
If I saw love in his eyes
That remind me of the beauty of Pacific blues.
I only half jest about all his well earned clout;
His majestic form is far surpassing the norm.
But it's the set of his jaw, and his beautiful smile.
His intelligence, warmth, and intentions;
Devoid of guile.
I've been acquainted with him mere moments
but my soul feels like we've been
Intertwined for a lifetime.
I want to lay in his arms and reminisce

about the years we have ahead.
But for now I'll have to settle for the love
We share when I'm asleep in my bed.

INFINITY & BEYOND

I stare into those eyes and swear
They are the pair that can repair
every heartache, all the damage in the rear
View mirror of my mind as I recline & rewind
Through years of broken hearted nights
Unrelenting fights but then fear comes to rear
It's ugly head and the idea
That by your accounting I'm in arrears.
The interest is just not there
It's mathematically impossible for me to appear
To add up to the woman
you can see yourself with for years.
All deference to myself,
I'm a wealth of untapped potential.
And you've always managed to just smile
and I feel special.
Is it true, you may be feeling the same?
There's no shame in having doubts.
But me and you share something beautiful.
We can figure this out.
I know that neither of us really
believe in romance
Still I have a feeling that if
simply given the chance
We'd advance exponentially. Eventually
We could grow together
Just give me a sign that I'm not wasting my time

'Cause in my mind I do the math and realize
I could love you forever.

GRAVE OF DREAMS

Here I lie.
Old enough but not quite old ... enough.
So much potential.
A life well lived?
Unsure. But definitely eventful.
Is the totality of my existence
Measured only in time?
Only in accomplishments or prestige?
The fights I lost, the battles I won?
All of it leading to this plot of
Nothingness. The big sleep.
Dreams I have yet to fulfill.
Places I haven't yet traveled to-
All gone because I did not take time
To make time? That doesn't sound right
It's just plain wrong.
The flesh is so weak
But my mind was quite strong.
No, it is quite strong.
Lying here defeated is not where I belong.
They never gave up on me, so why should I?
I may not be all they expected, but I can try
To rise to the occasion and learn to fly.
Keep building, keep growing
Keep failing until I succeed.
Though success to me may be
Of a different breed.

Fame was never the objective;
I prefer my privacy.
I'm introverted, and kind, and hard on myself.
I am flawed, I am bruised, I take it all to heart
The past has entrapped me in
a prison of my mind.
But with help, with these words, I've come to find
A way out of the mire of this system of things.
Found love and support to pull me up.
Observed strength in my friends and family.
Tried to imitate the resolve I see in them.
Proud of the tradition of resilience I see.
So I lie in a grave of dreams no more.
There is so much for me in store.

NO PLACE LIKE HOME

It begins with a promise.
A safe space. A haven.
Shelter from the storm.
A place of peace and calm.
A heart that remains open.
A door that never closes.
You return here when nothing is right
When everything is wrong
And it never quite loses its warmth.
For some this is a structure.
A picket fence and security alarm.
For others it's two open arms
And assurances to keep you from harm.
Some say home is where the heart is.
Others say they earned their deepest scars there.
Confusion. Pain. They fall apart there.
For me, I compartmentalize that feeling
Of safety when my head is reeling.
I can return there and find rest.
Welcome there, even when I'm not my best.
I can honestly say there's
No better feeling known
Than that of knowing my heart is safe at home

WINNER'S CIRCLE

Victory can be much closer than it seems
When you're following a trail of broken dreams
There's a resiliency that builds as you persevere
Desire that burns brighter
With each hurdle you clear
Though weary you may feel as time drags on
Never seeing an end to the road you travel on
It's well worth the fight to hold on to the end
Though at times you feel as if
You simply can't fend
Off the crushing despair,
When you're gasping for air
Or simply a helping hand to aide you through
If you just close your eyes long enough to decide
Whether this is the course
That was chosen for you
It may seem unbearable, terrible and unfair
You may stumble and fall prey to deep despair
But for every failure
you may soon figure out how
To course correct and deflect
Those doubts you allowed
To seep in and convince you
That you've already lost
But know this- truly winning
Always comes at great cost

MARVELOUS

You saved my life
Although you didn't know it
It's a testament to your influence
That you touched this broken soul
Bringing color and vibrance to
A place once dull and faded
Restoring faith to an outlook
That became so damn jaded
You aided in helping me see
In 3-dimensional clarity
I heard, saw, and felt every storyline
I tasted the tears that I wept
Over cinematic arcs and felt
My heart expand with each
Utterance of honor, friendship & love
I delved into emotional tropes
Of all of the above
You filled me with a sense of
Childlike wonder
With each heartbreak my heart
Was torn asunder
You gave me a glimpse of hope
That I could withstand anything
All the harsh realities life could bring
And yet with each ending you reminded me
That a new beginning was on the way
Altered only through time and space

Infinite possibilities lie in front of me
Even if some paths ended in a twisted form
You gifted me foresight beyond the norm
Though my feet are firmly planted
My views are somewhat slanted
Through frames that may warp the scenery
Freeing my mind of the confines of time
Allowing me to reshape what I believe
I am eternally grateful for
The laughter and joy
The honesty, integrity
The dignity & poise
In those moments that life became too
Chaotic you quieted the noise
And I am here today because I hope
One day to do the same for someone else
Give them strength through sight & words
When they fail to find it in themselves
I aim to be what you've inspired in me
A person marvelous
In thoughtfulness
In words, and good deeds.

FRAGILE INVINCIBILITY

There are some days I awake
With a smile on my face.
At times it feels too few
And far apart.
There are others that
Melancholia imbued
Causes me to go
Forth and create art.
Times I'm sleep deprived
And giddy. Others well rested
And full of self pity.
A wild ride on the emotional rollercoaster
That we call existence.
Some days I'm affectionate and soft;
Offering a shoulder to lean,
An ear to hear.
Others, I'm trapped in a prison of my mind
Battling my own demons and fear
I can't always find the words to say that I'm
Terrified about my fate.
But I'd gladly give my life to protect
The ones I love, save them from all pain.
God, I wish those things I could articulate
I fear they won't understand until
It's too late.
So I leave a few precious gems to find-
Small, intimate glimpses into my mind,

And hope the sum total of my being be
A lesson in fragile invincibility.

HAPPILY EVER AFTER

Take another look at me.
Actually, don't look at me.
See me.
I'm not exactly who I aspired to be.
Had you told a younger version
Of me (from my teens) that
I'd be grown, single & carefree?
She wouldn't have believed you.
She was a girl with a head full of naiveté.
Her head was in the clouds, it seems.
She often thought that success was found
In others' expectations. Seriously.
If she knew the woman I'd become
Would find contentment in herself...
Would she be disappointed that in
Her 30's she hadn't acquired wealth?
Well, that's not quite true, if I'm being honest.
I found my treasure once
I began being honest about what
It was I truly wanted to accomplish.
I want to be heard.
I want my words to echo
Through the annals of history.
I want just one child to look me up
And find someone in whom they can believe.
I relish the thought of honoring my family.
But also to cast light in the dark places

Where I used to hide my misery.
I'm not special. I'm not grand,
But I fight and take a stand.
I refuse to lie supine and settle-
Letting others define who they think I am.
I am humbled each day
I'm blessed to open my eyes.
And for those who know me
It comes as no surprise
That I almost always try to find
A kind word to say. Evoke a smile.
Make you laugh, if only for a little while.
This world is so full of misery
So excuse me if I wish to be free
Of the burden of despair.
Take a breath of fresh air.
Revel in the melanated skin I'm in.
Dare to create, and never subjugate
To patriarchal archetypes and whims
I wish only to define the construct
Of a life that is wholly mine.
I find a deep appreciation and love
Of the divine Creator who found us
Worthy of being saved. And for those who
Seek it find a path that's paved
To a future much brighter than any of us
Could see on our own. Remind us that
We never have to feel alone.
So look at me now, but look to see

That I am sincerely, uniquely, thoroughly
Happy to be me.

33

C.C.

A tiny tempest
Tough as nails
Smart and fierce and all it entails
To being a well reckoned force, it's true
These qualities & more remind me of you
A tongue so sharp, with wit to match
Slices through any nonsense
With nary a hurt feeling intact
Firstborn bearing the heavy burdens
Of loving, living, learning from
A matriarch as beautifully complex
As the day is long
Growing up having to be so strong
Becoming the wise, brilliant, and bold
Mother & aunt who never seems to grow old
Though she may seem at times to be rigid
I can attest her heart has never been frigid
So let's give it up for this favorite auntie of mine
The incomparable C.C. - she's one of a kind